DR. STEPHEN SWIHART

3-T DISCIPLESHIP

• TOUCHING   • TEACHING   • TRAINING

MASTER PLAN MINISTRIES
Dr. Stephen Swihart • 1333 El Reno Street • Elkhart, IN 46516
Web: www.MasterPlanMinistries.com

Contents

Part One

BEHIND THE SCENES

Chapter One

"ONLY ONE THING"

Mary sat at the Lord's feet listening to what he said.
But Martha was busy with all the things that had to be done.
She came to Jesus and said, "Lord, my sister has left me
to do the work by myself. Don't you care? Tell her to help me!"
"Martha, Martha," the Lord answered.
"You are worried and upset about many things.
But only one thing is needed.
Mary has chosen what is better.
And it will not be taken away from her" (Luke 10:39-42, NIRV).

What **really** matters? Few people can answer that question accurately. We think love, peace, protection, provisions, family, success, and a thousand other things are important. And they are. But when compared to the **"one thing"** that really matters, they are all a distant second.

Therefore, before we engage in any conversation about discipleship, we must first major on the "one thing" that matters the most to the Lord. If we get this wrong, even a little bit, we will certainly miss the mark in the all-important work of making disciples.

The very first question we should ask ourselves is this: **What is more important than anything else?** Or, put another way,

What should be my number one priority every day for the rest of my life?

You would think that everyone should have this answer on the tip of their tongue, but the greater truth is that very few people can explain the "one thing" that should occupy the core of our life. Personally, I was a pastor and a seminary student working on my doctorate degree before I discovered the "one thing" that concerned the Lord more than anything else. I'll explain this point in a moment, but first, let's learn a lesson from two sisters.

One day, Martha, a close friend of Jesus, gladly invited him and his disciples into her home. Immediately, she busied herself with the important task of working in the kitchen to prepare a meal for everyone. But something unexpected happened: Mary didn't show up to help her; instead, she simply sat down at Jesus' feet and listened to him speak. The longer she failed to return to the kitchen and help her sister, the more frustrated Martha became. Finally, she decided something had to be done — there was just too much work for her to do by herself. So she went to Jesus and demanded that he tell Mary to get up and help her!

Martha's request sounded reasonable. She was preparing a large meal, and she needed some help. But there was a problem, a really big one, and Martha couldn't see it, even though it was in plain sight.

You might imagine, like me, that Jesus would gently encourage Mary to return to the kitchen and help her sister with the chores that needed attention, but he didn't do that. Instead, he actually rebuked Martha! Why would he do that? Martha's heart was sincere enough, and her hands were fully engaged in serving the Lord, but Jesus put his finger on a common problem that has caused every servant of the Lord to stumble to one degree or another.

There are many things you will need to learn as a Christian, but this one item is more important than everything else. It is a lesson about priorities. Which comes first: the *work* of the Lord or the *Lord* of the work?

**Martha was devoted to the WORK of the Lord.
Mary was devoted to the LORD of the work.**

The difference between these two priorities is huge. Martha saw the *task* that was before her, but all the while she overlooked the *Teacher* from heaven who was seated in her living room! As a result of this oversight she grew frustrated with her sister and made a demand from Jesus that he would not honor.

Many believers have fallen precisely here: *they have become so preoccupied with the WORK of the Lord that they have unconsciously overlooked the LORD of the work!* Eventually, when that happens, they wear out, like Martha, and they begin to complain. But the Lord won't honor their petitions because they have confused *performance* with *priorities*. They have forgotten that *worship of the Lord* is more important than *work for the Lord!*

I had this problem in spades. In addition to pastoring a new church, I managed to add other good works to my busy schedule:

- Three times a week (Sunday morning, Sunday night and Wednesday night) I presented a lengthy and carefully prepared teaching to the church. Naturally, in addition to these meetings there were weddings, funerals, hospital calls, normal visits, and business meetings to attend.

- Five days a week I was responsible to broadcast a short message on the local Christian radio station.

- At the request from a publisher, I agreed to the hefty assignment of writing a commentary on the entire New Testament.

- Shortly after receiving this writing task, I was asked to produce a reference book on end-time prophecy. I was given one month to finish the assignment, which I completed with great joy.

- Following the prophetic project came another one-month task: writing a reference book on angelology.

- Next, I had the "bright" idea to work on a doctorate degree. An elder in the church warned me that I might be biting off more than I could chew, but I dismissed his words because I was wholly devoted to the *work* of the Lord.

After two years of non-stop work, from the time I awoke until the time I fell asleep, something changed in my body. I couldn't think clearly, and my hands trembled without control. Eventually, I was unable to drive my car or even order food from a menu. That was the last straw. Reluctantly, I decided it was time to see a doctor. He ran a series of tests and asked me to return one week later.

When I went back to get the results from my family physician, he told me something I couldn't imagine: **"You have six months to live . . . unless you go home and do nothing!"**

"Do nothing!" I thought. I haven't any idea how to "do nothing," but I wasn't in a position to argue. I went home, spoke with my Elder Board, and received their permission to cut my workload in half. What a relief! But that was just the beginning. The Lord had some unexpected plans for me as well.

On July 16, 1984, I strongly sensed that the Lord was upset with my priorities. I have no other way to describe it: **He confronted me and told me that I had to change — period.** My days of putting the *work* of the Lord above the *Lord* of the work were over. No longer could I ignore God and replace Him with "spiritual" busyness. He wanted to fellowship with me, and He would see to it that it came to pass. I had no idea what that meant, but I was soon to find out, starting the very next morning.

It was early when the Lord woke me. I could hear His voice in my heart telling me to get up and go downstairs for devotions. Honestly, every cell in my body wanted to go back to sleep. The pillow was much more appealing to me at that hour than my Bible. Then I thought, "The *Lord* is waking me and urging me to join Him for devotions; why would I rather stay in bed?" So I asked Him just before getting up why I loved

sleeping more than entering His presence? This was His reply:
"Because your heart is rotten!" I was shocked, but He was right.

For the next nine months we had that kind of relationship:
I would ask questions, and He would tell me the truth that I
needed to hear. Some days the Lord would tell me not to ask
questions, but simply to take notes as He spoke to me about a
matter that was on his heart. In a short time I had a large stack
of life-changing "messages" from the Lord. Our relationship became so real there were times I actually thought He was seated
in the chair beside me! For three-fourths of a year I had almost
daily experiences similar to that of Moses who went to his "Tent
of Meeting" and fellowshipped with the Lord "face to face" (Ex.
33:7-11). Morning after morning the Lord kept showing up,
waking me and nudging my heart and urging me to meet with
Him. Eventually, I came to see my meetings with the Trinity as
my highest priority and joy! Slowly, but surely, my devotion to
the *work* of the Lord was being replaced with a higher priority:
meetings with the *Lord* of the work!

Without any doubt, the most important lesson I learned in
these intimate meetings is this: *God has more than ears to hear me
when I speak; He also has a mouth to speak to me if only I will listen!* It
took a few months for this fact to sink in, but I eventually came
to see that God genuinely wants to meet with me every time I
read His Word or pray! *In other words, mechanical devotions were
being replaced with actual meetings with the Lord himself!* From that
time forward I stopped going to the Bible or to prayer, instead
I learned to go to <u>God</u> via the Bible and prayer! That statement
may sound simplistic, but it has changed my entire life.

At last, I made a long overdue transition: my new priority
would not be the *work* of the Lord, but the *Lord* of the work. I
would sit at His feet, like Mary. I would pursue the "one thing"
that is more important than anything else — His presence! In
the thirty years that have followed these Divine encounters, I
have heard from the Lord via the Scriptures and the Spirit literally thousands of times! I am now at the place where I can tell
you that fellowship with the Lord is the most important part of
my daily life. It is the "one thing" Martha and I needed to learn

to value above all else. And it is the "one thing" you must learn to experience and treasure as well.

Therefore, before you engage in the work of making disciples of other people, you must first experience what it means to be discipled by the Lord himself! Why? Because discipleship is not ultimately about intense Bible studies or personal discipline or countless good deeds; it is about an intimate relationship with the living Lord of lords and King of kings!

---

1. In your own words, explain and illustrate the "one thing" that Jesus wants present in your life above everything else.

2. Your main mission in making disciples is to help people find and follow God (Father, Son and Holy Spirit) as intimately as possible. Discipleship is not about rules, but a vibrant and transforming relationship with God and people. Explain the difference between being devoted to the *work* of the Lord and the *Lord* of the work.

3. Based on your own experiences, how frequently and how deeply do you connect with God?

Chapter Two

EARS THAT HEAR HEAVEN

I don't speak on my own authority.
The Father who sent me has commanded me
what to say and how to say it . . .
I say whatever the Father tells me to say" (John 12:49-50, NLT).

Throughout your study and practice of discipleship, you should keep in the forefront of your mind the lesson we learned from Mary and Martha:

The WORK of the Lord is important.
The LORD of the work is more important.

At its core, discipleship is not about prayer, Bible study, church attendance, witnessing, service projects or character development. Instead, it is primarily about knowing God (Father, Son and Spirit) intimately. It is out of this heart-to-heart relationship that genuine discipleship is birthed. In other words, *worship* comes before *work,* just as *meeting with God* comes before *ministry with people.*

Honestly, this is where most of us get stuck. We agree with the above paragraph, but then we go on reading the next paragraph without any serious pause or heart inspection. We say with our *lips* that spending quality time with God is critical, but with our *lives* we are easily side-tracked. Right? We are all better at "talking the talk" than we are at "walking the walk." That's why we need to look to Jesus. His *talk* and his *walk* were in perfect alignment. Only he can show us how to make the transition from *sincerity* to true *spirituality!*

When you read the four Gospels (Matthew, Mark, Luke and John), you discover that Jesus practiced the "one thing" he urged Martha to make her top priority. He didn't begin and end his days with the *work* of the Father, but with the *Father* of the work!

For example, early in the morning, before dawn, Jesus could be found in prayer (Mk. 1:35). At the end of the day, Jesus could also often be found seeking God in private (Mt. 14:23; Lk. 6:12). *While he spent a great deal of time engaged in ministry to people, his first and final priority every day was to spend time in meetings with his Father.* This was the "secret" to Jesus' remarkable success!

Jesus learned something that all disciples must learn if they are going to be effective: *he became skillful in hearing from his Father.* Prayer, for Jesus, was not a matter of going through a list of names and needs, but an opportunity to unload his heart before God and then to wait patiently while God unloaded His own heart. This sort of praying wasn't mechanical monologue, but fresh, vibrant, enlightening and transforming dialogue. It was in this atmosphere that he and the Father conversed back and forth about everything. In fact, this daily dialogue was so important that Jesus insisted we personally regard it as our own daily diet: *People do not live by bread alone, but by every word that comes from the mouth of God (Mt. 4:4, NLT)!*

This revelation is so important that you must repeat it to yourself over and over and over, until it leaves your head, enters your heart, and transforms your whole life! This is the way Jesus lived, and it is the way we must learn to live as well. Jesus began his mornings with the Father, and he ended his evenings again with the Father. It was this pair of "prayer bookends" that gave him his power throughout the day. As a result of this special fellowship, he grew to realize that he could hear from God anywhere and at any time.

Let me show you, in Jesus' own words, how his entire life and ministry were supernaturally empowered because of his special intimacy with his Father. When you read the following passages, picture Jesus listening to His Father's voice. Then envision yourself doing the same thing.

- Jesus told the people: "I tell you for certain that the Son cannot do anything on his own. He can do only what he sees the Father doing, and he does exactly what he sees the Father do" (Jn. 5:19, CEV).

- "I can do nothing on my own. I judge as God tells me. Therefore, my judgment is just, because I carry out the will of the one who sent me, not my own will" (Jn. 5:30, NLT).

- "I have much to say about you and much to condemn, but I won't. For I say only what I have heard from the one who sent me, and he is completely truthful." But they still didn't understand that he was talking about his Father.

  So Jesus said, "When you have lifted up the Son of Man on the cross, then you will understand that I Am he. I do nothing on my own but say only what the Father taught me. And the one who sent me is with me — he has not deserted me. For I always do what pleases him." Then many who heard him say these things believed in him (Jn. 8:26-30, NLT).

- "I did not speak of my own accord, but the Father who sent me commanded me what to say and how to say it. I know that his command leads to eternal life. So whatever I say is just what the Father has told me to say" (Jn. 12:49-50, NIV).

- "The very words I say to you are not my own. It is the Father who lives in me who carries out his work through me" (Jn. 14:10b, PHILLIPS).

- "The words you hear me say are not my own. They belong to the Father who sent me" (Jn. 14:24b, NIRV).

I cannot count the number of times I have read these verses. In fact I have marked these passages in my Bible so I can quickly and easily go through the list. At the end of John 5:19, I have written "5:30." After John 5:30, I have jotted down "8:26-28." And so on. It would be a good idea for you to follow this same practice. *Let me earnestly suggest that you prayerfully read these verses every day for at least two weeks.* If you will take this assignment seriously, there is a high likelihood that your sensitivity to God's presence and voice will increase dramatically!

How rarely do we sit-and-soak in God's presence. We are better at splashing and dashing. We convince ourselves that there are more urgent things to do than sit patiently at the feet of God the Father, God the Son and God the Spirit. Too often we believe that being sincere and busy in the Lord's work will accomplish God's will, but we are mistaken. God isn't looking for people with good motives and good work habits! *Instead, He is searching for people with good ears, people who know how to listen to Him any time and at any location (Mt. 11:15; Heb. 3:7ff; Rev. 2:7, 11, 17, 29; 3:6, 13, 22; etc.).*

If there is one city in the world where Christians take the call to meet with God seriously it would be Seoul, South Korea. It is common for churches there to conduct one to two hour prayer meetings every weekday, starting at 5:00 a.m. In addition, some churches add an all-night prayer meeting every Friday. On Sundays it is normal for believers to spend one hour or more in prayer before the services begin. Everything is saturated in prayer. The Christians there have not only learned how to pray, but how to live in prayer. For them, prayer is the most important part of their lives!

Does this kind of devotion to prayer make a difference? Consider a few results. In 1950, only 8% of the population in South Korea was Christian. Today, it is more than 30%! Every Sunday, prayer-filled churches preach the gospel and literally thousands come to Christ! *In one particular church (Yoido Full*

Gospel Church) an average of 12,000 people pray to become Christians every month! This sort of evangelism doesn't happen in a prayer-less atmosphere. Instead, it is the result of pastors and ordinary Christians who believe that meeting with God is their highest duty and honor!

When we look at the church in America, is it any wonder we find so little spiritual fruit? According to researchers, 80% of all the churches in the United States have either plateaued or are in a state of decline! Let's take a closer look. Examine the prayer hab-its of most congregations and Christians. Extensive surveys have discovered that the average believer in the United States spends just 3-7 minutes daily in prayer! Even worse, the average church has discontinued weekly prayer meetings! Can you connect the dots here? In South Korea, believers pray fervently, and tens of thousands of their fellow citizens are becoming converts. In the United States, believers barely pray at all, and very, very few people in our nation are being saved.

If we will be completely honest, we will have to admit that many professing Christians in our nation are more sincere than spiritual, more busy than fruitful, more defensive than transparent, more lazy than earnest, and more distracted than focused! Very few of us practice the "one thing" Jesus requires. Honestly, only a small percentage of Christians in North America actually live in the "one thing" that Jesus and Mary experienced. It is this fact that explains why most believers and churches in our area of the world know very little about the Great Commission and the practice of making disciples. Like the members of the church at Ephesus, we know how to work and even persevere, but we do not know how to live in "first love" (or the "one thing;" see Rev. 2:1-7).

The point here is this: if you or your church wishes to be ef-fective in making disciples, then you must first learn, like Jesus, how to hear from God and how to depend on every word He speaks!

- In a very practical way explain the "secret" behind Jesus' success.

- Did you mark the passages in John's gospel where Jesus discusses his ability to hear his Father's voice? And have you reviewed these passages daily for your own improvement in prayer?

- If the Lord were in full control of your prayer habits, what would he compliment, and what would he change? Be specific.

- How will you teach your family and others the way to have ears that hear from heaven?

Chapter Three

CHANGE PRODUCES CHANGE

"Here I am! I stand at the door and knock.
If anyone hears my voice and opens the door,
I will come in and eat with him, and he with me . . .
He who has an ear, let him hear
what the Spirit says to the churches" (Revelation 3:20, 22, NIV).

It's tucked away in a single verse, almost hiding in plain sight. It's the account of God visiting the Garden of Eden in the cool of the day (literally, in the "breeze" of the day, which was in the late afternoon and early evening hours). This visit isn't presented as an unexpected appearance, but a common one, likely a daily occurrence: *They [Adam and Eve] heard the sound of the Lord God walking in the garden in the cool of the day (Gen. 3:8, ESV).*

Can you visualize it? The day's work is finished. It's time to sit down to the main meal of the day. It's time to relax. It's time to catch your breath. It's time to be brought up to speed on what's been happening with the rest of the family. And there's more: it's also time for God to visit your dining room for food and fellowship! What an amazing way to spend an evening!

In commentaries and theological books you learn that these kinds of appearances of God in the Old Testament are called *theophanies*. Technically, they were appearances of *God the Son*. The Bible simply states that "God" or the "Lord" or "the angel of the

19

Lord" showed up, and He did so in the outward form of an ordinary man (see Gen. 16:7-18; 18:1-33; 31:11-12; 48:15-16; Exod. 3:2-6; 23:20-21; Jdg. 2:1-5; 6:11-24; Dan. 3:25-28; etc.). At this point in history, God the Son was not a human, so He took on the "image" of a man so Adam and Eve could easily and comfortably communicate with Him.

Imagine it. Jesus repeatedly appears in the Old Testament, and he looks like the man he will eventually become when he takes on our humanity! And what does he do in his earliest appearances? He simply, and profoundly, talks with Adam and Eve. He spends time with them. Apparently, he even eats with them. For an hour, maybe two, he just sits, listens, and talks with them. It is fellowship at the highest possible level!

Later, in the New Testament, Jesus actually leaves heaven, comes to earth, and takes on our humanity. He becomes a man! Yes, Jesus continued to be fully God, but in some remarkable miracle he also became fully man: the one, the only, God-Man.

As a man we see Jesus doing what he did many years earlier: he spends time with people, including eating and drinking with them. This habit of Jesus was so common that his enemies accused him of being a glutton and a drunk (Matt. 9:10-11; 11:19)! But Jesus let this charge fall to the ground with a thud. He would take advantage of every opportunity to eat and talk with both saints and sinners (Mt. 14:15-21; Mk. 7:1ff; 8:1-9; Lk. 7:36-50; 10:38-42; 14:1-24; 19:1-10; 24:28-31, 35-43; Jn. 2:1-11). In fact, at one point Jesus personally prepared breakfast and invited his disciples to eat with him (Jn. 21:1ff).

After the death and resurrection of Jesus you would expect that his days of eating and conversing were over, but this isn't so. In fact, he encourages his followers to open the door of their home and heart and invite him in for fellowship. Listen to Jesus request the pleasure of dining with you: *"Look! I stand at the door and knock. If you hear my voice and open the door, I will come in, and we will share a meal together as friends" (Rev. 3:20, NLT).*

In the late afternoon or early evening, when it's time to relax and sit down to a meal, Jesus knocks on your door. He wants to spend some time with you. Casual. Comfortable. Insightful. Burden-lifting. And more. This is what Jesus offers to all of us every day!

There is one more major reference to eating with Jesus that we cannot skip over. At the end of the present age, at the end of the world as we know it, Jesus will invite us to join him and his Bride (the true Church) for a very special meal:

> *Then I heard again what sounded like the shout of a vast crowd or the roar of mighty ocean waves or the crash of loud thunder:*
> *"Praise the Lord!*
> *For the Lord our God, the Almighty, reigns.*
> *Let us be glad and rejoice, and let us give honor to him.*
> *For the time has come for the wedding feast of the Lamb, and his bride has prepared herself.*
> *She has been given the finest of pure white linen to wear."*
> *For the fine linen represents the good deeds of God's holy people."*
> *And the angel said to me, "Write this: Blessed are those who are invited to the wedding feast of the Lamb." And he added, "These are true words that come from God" (Rev. 19:6-9, NLT).*

Sometime in the future, after the second coming of Christ, all of God's children will join Jesus for the grandest meal of them all — it will be his "wedding feast!" Every believer, from Adam to the last soul who surrenders his or her heart to Christ, will dine together and celebrate our profound marriage to Jesus!

There are at least two colossal points to be made from all of the above information:

- One, Jesus loves people; he loves you, and he wants to spend time with you, especially at the end of every day. He isn't too busy to listen to the cry of your heart — never! It is his favorite part of every day: listening to you and sharing his own insights in return. Fellowship. That's a mighty big word in Jesus' vocabulary. This is much more than a Bible study; it is a relationship, a real, heart-felt relationship.

- Two, our highest honor and joy every day should be to spend time with God (Father, Son and Spirit). If prayer is dull or a burden, then it is clear that we don't see our time with Him as He views it. Prayer — real prayer — isn't about talking and informing the Lord of things He already knows. *The heart of prayer is the prayer of the heart.* It is entering His presence; it is being still and soaking in the attributes of His grace, power, love, holiness, sufficiency, compassion, wisdom, discernment, and more. It is all about mingling, interweaving, merging and meshing your thoughts and feelings with His very own nature. It is about partnership. It is about becoming "one" with the Lord Almighty. It is about that "one thing" that no one else can enjoy but a son or daughter of the King of kings!

Words can only take you so far. And in the presence of God words can even get in the way. Sometimes you will need music. Not loud music. Not bouncy music. Not hand-clapping music, but hand-raising music. Worship — deep soulful music — can take you where words cannot go. That explains why the Psalmists (and others) urge us, again and again, to sing and make music in our hearts before the Lord (Psa. 27:6; 33:2; 81:2; 92:1; 95:2; etc.). Honestly, your worship of God with music should not be limited to Sunday mornings in church. It is also a good practice to spend time soaking in worship and meditating on God any time of the day or night.

How many songs do you have on an electronic device that actually help you submerge yourself in God's presence? Again, I am not speaking simply about the kinds of songs that you like to hear or sing. I am referring to a deeper sort of music. I am talking about the type of music that literally assists you in finding the heart of God, music that uplifts and heals, music that turns words into worship.

Every now and then everyone should take an hour (or longer) to be bathed in good music — the best of the past and the best of the present. For me, that means songs like these: *Softly and Tenderly; Come Holy Spirit; Because He Lives; Holy, Holy, Holy; I Stand in Awe; I'd Rather Have Jesus; Turn Your Eyes Upon Jesus; In the Garden; Through It All; and hundreds more.* Classic songs. Contemporary songs. All of the best songs you can find to help you worship the Lord.

Nothing will help you more than learning to enjoy God's presence in His Word, in prayer, and in worship music. *Honestly, we have too much music and too little worship in our homes and churches!* We need more and more vertical fellowship. We need to open our door and invite Jesus in for a meal . . . for an entire evening!

The level of your fellowship with people depends on the level of your fellowship with Jesus. When you learn how to give to and receive from the Godhead, then (and only then) are you prepared to give to and receive from fellow disciples. Making disciples isn't about following rules, being disciplined, reading page after page of Scripture, or praying about people and problems. Making disciples is about developing a relationship that reflects your relationship with God: transparent, honest, humble, joyful, convicting and transforming. Discipleship is about experiencing (and helping others experience) the "one thing" that matters the most to the Lord!

One of the greatest lessons I have ever learned about making disciples is this: *It isn't what you "preach" that makes a difference; it's what you "practice" that carries weight.* People are far more impressed with an *example* than they are with an *explanation*.

If you want to be used by the Lord to make a difference in someone's life, then you must allow the Lord first to make a difference in your own life! *In other words, when you permit the Lord to work in you and to change you, then he will be glad to work through you in order to change others.* Here's the basic formula of discipleship: *To the degree that I am prepared to let the Lord change me, I am prepared to let the Lord use me.*

Permit me to say it another way: *It takes a changed person to change another person!*

Before Jesus sent out his disciples to make other disciples, he first had to change them. And before you can make the kind of disciples Jesus wants, he will have to change you as well. The main reason so many believers today do not reproduce themselves and make other disciples is due to the single fact that they have yet to be adequately changed by Christ; they have yet to abandon their own will and pick up the will of God to make disciples.

All too often we mistakenly imagine that if we can get people to attend church and some classes they will grow up spiritually and reproduce themselves. But the facts are against us: 95% of all believers never give birth to another believer! We can do better than that; we must!

- When's the last time you spent an entire evening with Jesus? If it has been quite a while, fix a date and set everything aside for an in-depth One-on-one with the Lord. Make it a habit.

- When's the last time in God's presence your "words" were turned into "worship?" Describe how your times of worship have impacted your life.

- Have you experienced the power of worship music? I am not referring to "enjoying" Christian songs, but using music skillfully in order to sit-and-soak in God's presence? Explain your experience. Also, identify a few of the songs that quickly draw you upward and into the heart of God.

- Finally, is the Lord changing you? How?

Part Two

3 - T DISCIPLESHIP

Chapter Four

TOUCHING PEOPLE

> *When Jesus came down from the mountainside,*
> *large crowds followed him.*
> *A man with leprosy came and knelt before him and said,*
> *"Lord, if you are willing, you can make me clean."*
> <u>*Jesus reached out his hand and touched the man*</u>.
> *"I am willing," he said. "Be clean!"*
> *Immediately he was cleansed of his leprosy (Matthew 8:1-3).*

Everywhere Jesus went, every day of the week, one thing was constant: *he would touch people . . . he would touch them with power . . . and he would touch them with compassion.*

There was no secret to Jesus' approach to ministry: *it was abundantly obvious that he had a powerful connection with God, and it was equally plain that he had a deep compassion for people. The constant aim of his ministry was to bring these two passions together.*

Power with God and compassion for people, this was the distinctive feature behind every work and word of Jesus. Read the four Gospels (Matthew, Mark, Luke and John); on one page after another there is example after example of both dynamic power and compelling compassion.

1. Touched by Compassion

The average Jew in Jesus' day received little help from the religious leaders. Instead, they made any attempt at pleasing God more and more difficult with one man-made rule after another. Jesus said of them, *They crush people with unbearable religious demands and never lift a finger to ease the burden (Matt. 23:4, NLT)!*

On the other hand, Jesus offered everyone a refreshing and comfortable relationship with God. It wouldn't be about endless and senseless rules, but about grace, freedom and fulfillment. Listen to Jesus' invitation to walk with God: *Are you tired? Worn out? Burned out on religion? Come to me. Get away with me and you'll recover your life. I'll show you how to take a real rest. Walk with me and work with me—watch how I do it. Learn the unforced rhythms of grace. I won't lay anything heavy or ill-fitting on you. Keep company with me and you'll learn to live freely and lightly (Matt. 11:28-30, Message).*

Jesus offered people truth mixed with grace. He gave them hope and joy. He helped them find peace in the midst of a world filled with chaos. He loved them, and they knew it. Listen to the heart of Jesus in the following passages.

- *Jesus went through all the towns and villages . . . When he saw the crowds, <u>he had compassion on them</u>, because they were harassed and helpless, like sheep without a shepherd (Matt. 9:35-36).*

- *When Jesus landed [on the beach] and saw a large crowd, <u>he had compassion on them</u> and healed their sick (Matt. 14:13-14).*

- *Jesus called his disciples to him and said, "<u>I have compassion for these people</u>; they have already been with me three days and have nothing to eat. I do not want to send them away hungry, or they may collapse on the way." He told the crowd to sit down on the ground. Then he took the seven loaves and the fish, and when he had given thanks, he broke them and gave them to the disciples, and they in turn to the people. They all ate and were satisfied (Matt. 15:32-36).*

- *As Jesus and his disciples were leaving Jericho, a large crowd followed him. Two blind men were sitting by the roadside, and when they heard that Jesus was going by, they shouted, "Lord, Son of David, have mercy on us!" Jesus had compassion on them and touched their eyes. Immediately they received their sight and followed him (Matt. 20:29, 34).*

- *A man who had a skin disease came to Jesus. On his knees he begged Jesus. He said, "If you are willing to make me 'clean,' you can do it." Jesus was filled with deep concern. He reached out his hand and touched the man. "I am willing to do it," he said. "Be 'clean'!" Right away the disease left him. He was healed (Mk. 1:40-42, NIRV).*

Why did so many people from so many places, day after day, want to be close to Jesus . . . to see everything he did and to hear everything he said? Because Jesus was different, in a good way. He loved people from the heart. He truly cared. And the people responded with appreciation.

Throughout church history there have been a good number of people and organizations that have displayed this remarkable kind of compassion: World Vision, Compassion International, Operation Blessing, Prison Fellowship, Teen Challenge, Feed the Hungry, Samaritan's Purse, Christian Aid Ministries, Feed the Children, Baptist World Aid, World Compassion, and hundreds of others.

One remarkable example is found in the life and works of William Booth (1829-1912). As a young man he knew God was calling him to preach the gospel of Jesus Christ, but not in the ordinary way. Booth's heart was profoundly impacted by the desperate needs he saw among the poorest of the poor people in London. His heart was so taken by their plight that in 1865 he began "The Christian Mission." He worked tirelessly to help the most needy in the city, including alcoholics, criminals and pros- titutes. He also opened kitchens to feed those who had no way to feed themselves. His ministry eventually became well known for offering people three S's: *soup, soap and salvation.* In a short while Booth's movement took on this motto: *Heart to God, Hand to Man.* With one hand they reached upward; with the other hand they reached outward.

It wasn't long before this ministry attracted volunteers, and a "light" was beginning to shine in the darkest regions of England. In 1867, Booth had just ten full-time workers. Seven years later that number grew to 1,000 volunteers with around 100 full-time evangelists and 75 mission stations. Every passing year brought more people eager to reach the lost and the hurting. By the time of Booth's death in 1912, he had traveled five million miles for the gospel, preached 60,000 sermons, and recruited 16,000 leaders to his "Salvation Army" (a title they developed in 1878). At his death, 150,000 people filed past his coffin, while another 40,000 attended his funeral, including Queen Mary.

Today, the Salvation Army has outreaches in 126 nations with more than 1,100,000 "soldiers" in their service. They have numerous hostels for the homeless around the world, including special centers for children, the elderly, and mothers with babies. And all of this is accomplished while focusing on its worldwide mission to preach the gospel of Jesus Christ and to meet human needs in His name without discrimination.

How does the Salvation Army or any church or any Christian actually make a difference in the world? This is the answer, the only answer: by caring, by getting involved, by loving people — spirit, soul and body, by the power of God.

It's an old saying, but it remains 100% true today: *People don't care how much you know until they first know how much you care!* Repeat this sentence several times to yourself. Let it sink in deeply, until it becomes a new and fresh standard for your own spiritual work.

If you are going to become effective in making disciples, you must first and foremost become a people-person . . . you must genuinely love the people you seek to impact . . . you must sincerely desire to help them — in spirit, soul and body. Anything less than this is an unprepared heart. And an unprepared heart has yet to be broken by the things that break the heart of God.

2. Touched by Power

Jesus did more than touch people with *compassion;* he also touched them with *power.* He literally did things no one else could do; he performed miracles by means of the Spirit working in his life (Matt. 12:28; Lk. 4:1, 16-21; 5:17; Acts 10:37-38; etc.)! And these miracles were like supernatural magnets that attracted people with every sort of background and problem. Everyone wanted to be *touched* by Jesus' power. And he did not disappoint them.

Notice in the following passages how Jesus was anointed to help people supernaturally. Read these verses slowly. Visualize him in your mind as he stretches out his hands to *touch* people with power.

- Jesus shockingly places his healthy hands on a man with an ugly and dreaded skin disease, leprosy (Matt. 8:1-3).

- Jesus lovingly holds the hand of Peter's mother-in-law as she lays in bed sick with a fever (Matt. 8:14-15).

- Jesus tenderly touches and heals the eyes of various men who are blind (Matt. 9:27-30; 20:29-34; Mk. 8:22-26).

- Jesus places his gentle hands on the heads of children and prays the Father's blessing on them (Mk. 10:13-16).

- Jesus, with deep concern, lays his hands on numerous sick people and heals them (Mk. 6:4-6a).

- Jesus casts demons from a youth who collapses and seems to pass out. But Jesus reaches out his hand to help him get up and return him to his overwhelmed father (Mk. 9:14-27).

- Jesus tenderly stops a funeral service by placing his hands on the defiled coffin and telling the youth inside to "get up" (Lk. 7:11-15). The young man immediately rises and begins to speak! Jesus then returns this teenager to his joy-filled mother.

- Jesus touches the small hand of a young girl who is thought to be dead. Instantly, she wakes up and is restored to health (Lk. 9:23-25).

- Jesus stretches out his hand to rescue Peter as he is about to sink under the fierce waters in the Sea of Galilee (Matt. 14:22-33).

- Even on the night of Jesus' arrest, when a member of the mob has his ear whacked off by Peter, Jesus places his anointed hand on the injured man's head and restores his ear (Lk. 22:49-51).

- In a summary statement by Peter, this is the way he described Jesus and his ministry: *You know the story of what happened in Judea. It began in Galilee after John preached a total life-change. Then Jesus arrived from Nazareth, anointed by God with the Holy Spirit, ready for action. He went through the country helping people and healing everyone who was beaten down by the Devil. He was able to do all this because God was with him (Acts 10:37-38, The Message).*

In story after story Jesus is seen touching people with an anointing of *compassion* and *power*. It was this supernatural enablement that set Jesus apart and made him effective. Understanding this fact is crucial! Why? Because experiencing a similar anointing of compassion and power will be necessary in order for you to have a truly Christ-like ministry!

Honestly, far too much of what we do for the Lord, both individually and corporately, is performed in our own strength and with our own human resources. We have substituted *the Spirit's work* with *our own sincerity.* We have mostly forgotten how to rely on God for supernatural words and works. Many people today are weary of church-as-usual because there is no clear evidence that Jesus is showing up with compassion and power. We have nearly *endless meetings;* what we need is *anointed ministry!*

If I have learned anything in more than four decades of ministry, it is this: *one experience with God is far better than 1,000 explanations about God!* In modern Christianity we have stressed the importance of a *Scriptural education,* and that's excellent. But we need to understand that this is not a replacement for *spiritual power and life-changing experiences!*

The plain truth is that many of our problems are too deep to be fixed with human sincerity and a knowledge of Bible facts. You will need more than that. You will need supernaturally imparted wisdom, compassion and power. You will need a Divine anointing; you will need miracles.

Let me give you an example. One Sunday, after I had preahed, I was introduced to a visitor. She asked me if I would pray for her because she had a constant pain in both ears. I agreed, but told her that I would only pray what God placed in my heart. (Rather than pray a sincere prayer from my own heart, I always try to pray a spiritual prayer that reveals what is in God's heart.). With that statement, I closed my eyes and instantly heard the Lord tell me to pray that this woman would get another job. I had no idea what that mean, but that's exactly what I prayed. When I finished and looked up, it was quite obvious that this woman was not the least bit pleased with my prayer. Off she went to the front door and to her car.

One week later this lady returned to church. As she came through the front door, her eyes connected with mine. It was obvious she wanted to speak with me. When we got together, this is what she said:

> *Do you remember how you prayed for me last week? You asked the Lord to give me a different job. Well, I work at a factory where there is constant loud noise caused by metal colliding against other metal. My ears can't take it, and that's why they hurt all of the time. At 8:05 am Monday morning my boss came over and said he had a different job for me! He took me to a department where there was no clanging metal; it was quiet and peaceful. Pastor, I just want you to know that*

the pain in my ears is completely gone. Thanks for praying the way the Lord directed you and not the way I wanted!

Over the years, I have had many experiences like that. Of course, I don't always know how to pray, and I don't always see a miracle take place, but literally hundreds of times I have heard the Lord tell me what to do, what to say, and how to pray. I have come to depend on it.

I honestly do not believe that being sincere is enough. I want more, and I need more. With all of my being I want the Lord to work through me. That's why I pray daily for supernatural insights and Divinely empowered ministry. Even when I eat out with someone or when I have my family over, I pray for God's compassion and power to work through me. Truthfully, once you experience the *supernatural* you will be thoroughly dissatisfied with only the *natural*.

This is the way the early church prayed. They understood how weak they were in themselves; they knew they needed help from above if they were going to do God's work effectively. So they prayed for God's hands to join their own hands when they were engaged in ministry. They earnestly sought God to overcome their fear of persecution and to enable them to witness boldly in Jesus' name. Listen to them pray:

> *"Now, Lord, consider their threats and enable your servants to speak your word with great boldness. Stretch out your hand to heal and perform signs and wonders through the name of your holy servant Jesus."*
> *After they prayed, the place where they were meeting was shaken. And they were all filled with the Holy Spirit and spoke the word of God boldly (Acts 4:29-31).*

This is the way the first Christians prayed; this is the way today's Christians need to pray! Let's be real: most Christians and churches today do not understand supernatural ministry or deep prayer — the kind of prayer that cries out for courage to witness, the kind of prayer that pleads for miracles, the kind of prayer that results in people being filled with the Holy Spirit!

When Jesus engaged in ministry, he touched people tremendously with two things: the *compassion* and the *power* of God. When you engage in ministry, you will need a similar anointing of compassion and power.

It doesn't matter if you are a pastor, a church board member, a small group leader, a conscientious parent, a student, an employee, a neighbor, a friend or someone else. You need power you do not have in yourself. And that is precisely why the Lord wants to give you both *spiritual fruit* (love, joy, peace, patience, kindness, goodness, faithfulness, gentleness and self-control) and *spiritual gifts* (see Romans 12:6-8; 1 Corinthians 12:7-11, 28-31; Ephesians 4:11-13). These are supernatural anointings, and we should seek them until we know how to operate in them on a regular basis!

Let's take an honest look at our hearts, homes and churches:

- *Are we really hungry for Jesus to work with us, in us and through us (Matt. 28:19-20; Mk. 16:19-20)?*

- *Are we really relying on miracles instead of natural abilities and resources?*

- *Are we really making a life-changing difference in peoples' lives?*

- *Are we really winning people to Christ every year?*

- *Are we really training families to be sold out for the cause of discipleship — evangelism and edification?*

- *Are we really training people to know God both academically and experientially?*

- *Are we really able to prove to people that Jesus means more to us than anyone and anything else?*

- *Are we really eager to grow in Christ-centeredness, character and competence?*

- *Are we different — really different — from non-Christians and most "Christians" in our desires, decisions and daily priorities?*

WE ARE CONSTANTLY ON A STRETCH,
IF NOT A STRAIN, TO DEVISE NEW METHODS,
NEW PLANS, NEW ORGANIZATIONS
TO ADVANCE THE CHURCH AND SECURE
ENLARGEMENT AND EFFICIENCY FOR THE GOSPEL.
THE CHURCH IS LOOKING
FOR BETTER METHODS;
GOD IS LOOKING FOR BETTER MEN!

WHAT THE CHURCH NEEDS TODAY
IS NOT MORE MACHINERY OR BETTER,
NOT NEW ORGANIZATIONS
OR MORE AND NOVEL METHODS,
BUT MEN WHOM THE HOLY SPIRIT CAN USE
— MEN OF PRAYER,
MEN MIGHTY IN PRAYER.

THE HOLY SPIRIT
DOES NOT FLOW THROUGH METHODS,
BUT THROUGH MEN.
HE DOES NOT COME ON MACHINERY,
BUT ON MEN.
HE DOES NOT ANOINT PLANS,
BUT MEN — MEN OF PRAYER!

E. M. BOUNDS
"POWER THROUGH PRAYER"

Chapter Five

TEACHING PEOPLE

*When Jesus concluded his address,
the crowd burst into applause.
They had never heard teaching like this.
It was apparent that he was living everything he was saying
– quite a contrast to their religion teachers!
This was the best teaching they had ever heard
(Matthew 7:28-29, The Message)!*

Jesus was a teacher.

Everybody knows that.

But do you know why Jesus spent more time *teaching* than he did anything else?

The answer will surprise you. But first, let's not get ahead of ourselves. We must begin our investigation long, long ago. In a garden. With two figures: Eve and a serpent (Satan).

Satan's Number One Goal and Method

When you dig into the history of Satan, it becomes immediately obvious that he is far more than a corrupt and conspiring entity. He is also a mastermind of deception. With an outstanding intellect, he lies and tricks people into believing things that are not true and into doing things that are not good.

Satan's goal is to tamper with your mind so you will think the same way he thinks. He wants you to see matters from his point of view. He wants you to follow his will, not God's will. And the main method he will use to manipulate your mind is false teaching of one kind or another.

Let me say it until it sinks deeply into your heart: *Satan wants to deceive you, and he will use cleverly worded teachings to make you think his views are right and the Bible's statements are wrong (Jn. 8:44; Eph. 2:1-3; 2 Cor. 4:4; 11:13-5; 2 Tim. 2:25-26; 1 Pet. 5:8; 1 Jn. 5:19; Rev. 20:3, 8; etc.).* Study the manner in which the devil approached, deceived and defeated Eve. It is this progressive threefold trap that he has used millions and millions of times around the world to ruin peoples' lives. See if you can detect his strategy in the following verses.

> *Now the serpent was more crafty than any of the wild animals the Lord God had made. He said to the woman, "Did God really say, 'You must not eat from any tree in the garden'?"*

> *The woman said to the serpent, "We may eat fruit from the trees in the garden, but God did say, 'You must not eat fruit from the tree that is in the middle of the garden, and you must not touch it, or you will die.'"*

> *"You will not certainly die," the serpent said to the woman. "For God knows that when you eat from it your eyes will be opened, and you will be like God, knowing good and evil"* (Gen. 3:1-5).

Whoever controls you from your eyebrows up will also control you from your eyebrows down. (Visualize this picture in your mind.) Notice the three teaching points Satan used to overcome Eve (and so many others in the past as well as today).

- First, he puts *doubts* in her mind about the accuracy and authority of God's Word when he says, "Did God *really* say . . ." He questions the Word of God. Today, Satan does the same thing. He challenges the messages of the Bible. He puts *doubts* in the minds of people about the inspiration, the authority, and the accuracy of the Scriptures. He wants you to think for yourself. He wants you to question the teachings of His Book. This is where the fall begins. If the devil can get anyone to ponder the accuracy of the Bible, he is well on his way to ensnaring them in his trap.

- Second, he flatly *denies* God's Word when he says, "You will not certainly die!" This is a favorite teaching of the devil. He is quick to *deny* any teaching that God will judge people. According to Satan, God (if there is a God at all) loves people; He has prepared heaven for people; He will never judge people or send them to hell. This so-called God never wants people to feel guilty or abandoned or accountable. This made-up God is like a marshmallow, always soft and sweet. Satan's teaching about God bears little resemblance to the accurate teaching about God in the Bible.

- Third, he urges people to *disobey* God's Word when he says, "God knows when you eat from it [the forbidden tree] your eyes will be opened, and you will be like God . . . " In other words, God is withholding good things from people, but you can enjoy the good life, if you will simply *disobey* God's Word and do what your heart is telling you to do. Satan will do everything in his power to make God's commands look unappealing while making disobedience appear to be attractive and beneficial and fun.

Satan's *goal* is to keep you from believing, obeying and enjoying the truth of God's Word. His *method* is to trick you with phony *teachings* that contradict the actual truth. In fact, if he can, he will keep the messages of the Bible as far away from public schools, colleges, universities, government offices and the culture-at-large as possible. He does not want your mind to be filled with the truth. He wants you to believe his lies and join him in his ultimate destination: hell!

America's Fall from the Bible

On November 11, 1620, the first pilgrims landed on American soil. But before they set a single foot on their new land, they wrote and signed our original legislative document: *The Mayflower Compact.* Included in this historic and profound piece of literature are these momentous opening two lines: *In the name of God, Amen! We . . . have undertaken for the glory of God and the advancement of the Christian faith . . . a voyage to plant the first colony in the northern parts of Virginia.* America, from the instant of its inception, was founded for spiritual purposes.

Five years after establishing the Massachusetts Bay Colony, in 1635, the Puritans started in Boston the first elementary school supported by tax money. In 1647, they passed an ordinance which marked the beginning of the U. S. Public School system. At the center of its curriculum was the Bible!

Eighty-eight of the first 100 colleges founded in North America were organized for one reason: *to promote the gospel of the Lord Jesus Christ.* Every school founded in the colonies prior to the Revolutionary War (except the University of Pennsylvania) was established by some branch of the Christian church. All but two of the Ivy League schools were established for the primary purpose of training ministers in the gospel of Christ so every American and every Indian would be fully converted to Christ.

Harvard was the first college in America. It was created expressly for Christ and the Church. In 1646, Harvard adopted these rules: *(1) Everyone shall consider the main end of his life and studies to know God and Jesus Christ which is eternal life. (2) Seeing the Lord gives wisdom, everyone shall seriously, by prayer in secret, seek wisdom of Him. (3) Everyone shall so exercise himself in reading the Scriptures twice a day that they be ready to give an account of their proficiency.* By the end of the 1600's, some 52% of Harvard's graduates became ministers of the Christian gospel!

Yale was even more conservative. For over 100 years, from its inception in 1701 until well into the 19th century, it existed to exalt Christ. In 1814, Timothy Dwight, the President of the school, had this to say to his student body: *Christ is the only, the true, the living way of access to God. Give up yourselves therefore to him, with a cordial confidence, and the great work of life is done!*

The first President of Princeton said passionately, *Cursed be all learning that is contrary to the cross of Christ. Cursed be all learning that is not subservient to the cross of Christ!*

The college of William and Mary was begun "that the Christian faith might be propagated. Dartmouth was founded to train men as missionaries to the Indians. And on it went. For well over the first 200 years of our nation's history it was considered essential to keep Christ and Scripture as the backbone of all education.

Then, subtly and gradually, the attitude changed. Priorities shifted. Compromises to the Bible spread almost everywhere. Doubts about the accuracy and authority of God's Word were entertained. Long-held teachings of the Christian Faith were denied. Disobedience to God's commandments were tolerated and eventually accepted as normal. By the mid 20th century, God's Word was replaced with Satan's lies. The once-loved Bible is now one of the most-loathed books!

Martin Luther in the 1500's was right when he said, *I am much afraid that the universities will prove to be the great gates to hell, unless they diligently labor to explain the Holy Scriptures and to engrave them upon the hearts of youth. I advise no one to place his child where the Scriptures do not reign paramount. Every institution where men are not unceasingly occupied with the Word of God must become corrupt!*

Jesus' Number One Goal and Method

When you read the four Gospels (Matthew, Mark, Luke and John), you see Jesus in action. He is healing the sick, raising the dead, feeding the multitudes, casting demons out of people, walking on water, and much, much more. However, above all of these activities Jesus did one thing — one primary thing — over and over and over. This single occupation was more important to Jesus than anything else: *he was a teacher!* One hundred and five times Jesus was called a "teacher" and seen "teaching." Nothing else consumed him more than this one gift and responsibility: teaching.

Jesus' daily ambition was to reveal the truth to people so they could escape Satan's deception, and the method he used to open peoples' eyes was the method the devil used to close them: instruction.

In the letter of 1 John there is a profound sentence that must not escape your notice. John tells you in that sentence why Jesus came to earth: *The reason the Son of God appeared was to destroy the devil's work (3:8)!*

What was the devil's work? Deception.

What was Jesus' work? Truth.

How did Satan deceive people? By masquerading as an angel of light . . . by corrupting peoples' mind with phony teachings (see 2 Cor. 11:3, 13-15).

How did Jesus enlighten people? By teaching them God's Word . . . by proclaiming to them that man does not live by bread alone, but by every word that comes from the mouth of God (Matt. 4:4)!

The greatest gift you can give to every child, teenager and adult is the skillful teaching of the Bible in your home and in your church. There is no other way to shield your mind from Satan's deceit. Daily devotions in God's Word should be your highest priority!

- How often do you meet with the Lord through Bible reading, memorization and meditation?

- How skillfully have you trained your children and others to spend time in God's Book?

- How eager are you to attend in-depth Bible studies?

- How eager is your church to train you (preferably one-on-one) in skill of reading and studying the Scriptures? For instance, have you been taught the best ways to read and study the Bible?

How can a young man keep his way pure?
By living according to your word (Psa. 119:9).

I have hidden your word in my heart
that I might not sin against you (Psa. 119:11).

You have been born again . . .
through the living and enduring word of God.
Like newborn babies, crave pure spiritual milk [God's Word],
so that by it you may grow up in your salvation (1 Pet. 1:23; 2:2).

Chapter Six

TRAINING PEOPLE

*Jesus went up on a mountainside
and called to him those he wanted, and they came to him.
He appointed twelve that they might be with him
and that he might send them out to preach
and to have authority to drive out demons
(Mark 3:13-15).*

When you *touch* people, you literally impact them with the love and power of God. This is crucial, but it is not the end of your work, only the beginning. Next, you must *teach* people until their minds are so full of truth they can detect and overcome every falsehood they will encounter. This is imperative, but even then your work is not completed. You must also *train* people until they know how to pass on to others what they have been taught and experienced. In this final stage you actually prepare disciples of Christ to make additional disciples. This is the ultimate goal of discipleship: *helping people become mature in the Lord so they know how to make others mature in the Lord as well.*

Now visualize this process taking place in a home, between the parents and the children. First, Dad and Mom *touch* their children. They hold them, play silly games with them, provide for them and spend an abundance of time with them. They truly care, and it shows. But parenting (and discipleship) doesn't stop with love.

Next, good parents will *teach* their sons and daughters. They will be intentional in explaining over and over again what their children should believe and how they should behave. This will be a major priority in their daily lives. With tireless energy they will instruct their children in three primary matters: *Christ-centered living, character and competence.* Their home will be a school that is filled with daily *teachings.*

Last, concerned and mature parents will *train* their children until they see a spontaneous pattern of both vertical and horizontal obedience and love in their lifestyle. These parents do not merely *tell* their kids what they should do; they do not simply *take* them to church; instead, they assume the responsibility to *train* them until their sons and daughters both practice their faith and share it with others naturally.

This is the way the *home* is supposed to work, and it is the way the *church* is to work as well. In both of these places there should be an abundance of *touching, teaching and training!*

Jesus is Your Role Model

In the biblical text at the head of this chapter is a profound phrase. Notice that Jesus did not merely "call" or "appoint" twelve men. Instead, he specifically hand-picked these men so "they might be with him." Being "with" Jesus was a deeper level of association than merely being in the crowd in a particular location listening to Jesus speak. It involved being "with" Jesus in every location — in homes, on mountain sides, in synagogs, on the roads between towns, in olive groves overnight, and so on. Wherever Jesus went, the Twelve were to be "with" him. The Twelve disciples of Jesus were more than casual observers at a distance; they were intentional *trainees* who were to watch and listen to Jesus so closely that they could eventually duplicate what they saw and heard.

If there is anything the family and the church today has neglected, it is this essential practice of *with-ness* and *training* of others. We *talk* by the mile, but we normally *train* only by the inch. We need to open our eyes wide to recognize and reverse this practice!

I had my eyes opened when, as a college student, I became an assistant to my highly successful pastor. On the very first day of my job I rode with him to a Fire Station to meet and encourage some of the firemen (my pastor was the Chaplain of both the fire department and the police department). Next, we went to a private school to talk with the principal and encourage him (my pastor sometimes was a substitute teacher in this honors academy). After this, we went to the hospital for daily visits. Before we left the car, my pastor said, "We are going to visit a lady today who is ready to become a Christian. I want you to lead her to Christ." Really?! I wasn't ready for that assignment, but after making a few introductory comments, my pastor assisted me in leading this woman to the Lord, for real. The rest of the day we talked and visited with one person after another. By the end of "day one," I had an entirely new concept of the ministry. I watched. I listened. And I participated, admittedly at a very shallow level. After nearly five months of this "with" routine, my pastor said I was ready to be a student pastor. He wanted me to finish college and go to seminary, and that's exactly what I did. All of this became possible because my Pastor took *training* me seriously.

During the next forty years I earned a master's and a doctorate degree. I also managed to pastor several churches, be a Bible professor, and write about 100 books and booklets. More importantly, I continued the practice of meeting regularly "with" mature men of God for encouragement, wisdom, correction and transparent fellowship.

In recent years, I have had the privilege to become a mentor for some men who simply want to grow stronger in the Lord. One gentleman has come to my home three hours a week for the past four years. Another man comes once a month for around ninety minutes. A former student of mine and I meet monthly for breakfast, spiritual fellowship and to discuss a chapter from a book we read together. Until recently, a pastor and best friend of mine met monthly for three hours or longer in order to have heart-to-heart conversations. And so on. I believe strongly in "with" discipleship. I am convinced there is no other thing I have done that is more important than meeting with men on a regular basis in order for us to speak into one another's lives.

Anyone can be a parent or a pastor, but it takes a special person who can actually make a difference in someone's life — it takes a person who keenly understands how to *touch, teach and train* others in an intentional way!

The Primary Job of Every Church Leader

If you were to examine the lifestyle of many church leaders today you would probably think their primary jobs are to preach sermons, conduct weddings and funerals, cast vision for the congregation, and a thousand other little things. Certainly all of these duties have their place, but they are far from being "the primary job" of spiritual leaders. Let me show you what I mean. Paul identifies the leader's chief responsibility in Ephesians 4:11-13. Read this passage slowly, and see if you can spot it. Underline the key phrase that identifies the one thing every apostle, prophet, evangelist, pastor and teacher should do better than anything else.

> *Christ himself gave the apostles, the prophets, the evangelists, the pastors and teachers, to equip his people for works of service, so that the body of Christ may be built up until we all reach unity in the faith and in the knowledge of the Son of God and become mature, attaining to the whole measure of the fullness of Christ (Eph. 4:11-13).*

What did you underline? Here's the phrase that stands out for me: *to equip his people.* This is the leader's main task: *to equip people . . . to prepare people for spiritual ministry!*

If you think you can do that from the pulpit, you'd better look again at the way Jesus equipped people. He spent time "with" them. He *touched, taught and trained* them. I know I sound like a broken recording, saying the same thing over and over, but I refuse to get sidetracked. If you want to do heaven's work God's way and literally change lives, there is no better approach that will get it done!

48

Let's take an unusual look at Paul's words in Ephesians again. This time, examine his message in reverse order. Start at the end, and work your way back to the beginning. Start by noticing the ultimate goal of ministry: *maturity . . . the whole measure of the fullness of Christ.* This must be our target: developing a church that is full of spiritually mature men and women . . . a church that actually reflects the fullness of Christ.

Okay, but how do you achieve this lofty objective? Read backwards again. The church must first be *built up* and in *unity.* Alright, how does this come about? Continue reading in reverse order. The *people* [the people in the pew] are to make this happen . . . *they* are to engage in *works of service.* This is far more than passing out bulletins or collecting the offering. *The people* are to be actively involved in spiritual ministry; they are to touch, teach and train one another!

Let's not stop yet. Keep reading backwards. Here is the key to everything. In order for the people in the church to be used in bringing one another to spiritual maturity, they must first be *equipped* by the leaders of the church! Read it again: *Christ himself gave the apostles, the prophets, the evangelists, the pastors and teachers, to equip the body.*

The secret to a church's maturity and effectiveness depends on the starting point: *do the leaders in the church possess the skill and take the necessary time to be intentional about equipping every member?* Honestly, this isn't that hard to do, but it will never happen until each leader understands that this is his primary job, and that the growth of his church depends chiefly on this number one duty.

The regrettable truth is that most leaders in most churches are distracted by lesser responsibilities. In the end, they rarely equip and train future ministers because they are already overwhelmed with endless busyness. Consequently, they become convinced there simply isn't any time left to *train* people for spiritual ministry. But this is exactly the way Satan wants us to think. The actual truth is that there *is* time to touch, teach and train specific people, *if this is our priority!*

A Practical Way to Train Others

Look as long as you like, and you will finally come to the surprising conclusion that there simply is no exacting step-by-step program laid out for effective discipleship training in the Bible! Why not? Because the work of making disciples isn't a *program;* it's an *intentional and focused relationship!* You can only make mature disciples in the context of "with-ness," and the particular type of "with-ness" you will need will vary from person to person (or from small group to small group).

While *touching and teaching and training* will always be present in every equipping relationship, there is no single way to accomplish each of these facets. Therefore, there is a certain measure of freedom in approaching disciple-making. However, by observing the manner in which Jesus made mature and reproducing disciples who made other disciples, we can see in general terms a pattern that has proven to be effective century after century.

- First, Jesus spoke to large groups, sometimes filling a house or lining a mountain side.

- Second, Jesus hand-picked a few individuals for special training and ministry assignments. These disciples had greater access to him and therefore more opportunities to ask questions and be taught. They would be "with" him more than others.

- It was from this second group that new leaders emerged who were ready to equip others.

Here's the point. Attending church services and home Bible studies are good, but they are normally inadequate to make mature disciples who are able and willing to reproduce themselves. There are exceptions, of course, but by and large most people need more specialized attention (more homework, more ministry assignments and more accountability). This is why equipping-leaders, like Jesus, find and enlist a few good men into whom they can pour their hearts and minds with the intention of equipping them for ministry.

This is the way the apostle Paul did it with Timothy: *The things you [Timothy] have heard me [Paul] say in the presence of many witnesses entrust to reliable people who will also be qualified to teach others (2 Tim. 2:2).*

Carefully observe the sequence:

- Paul, a qualified equipping / training leader, selected Timothy to be his apprentice.

- Timothy, a trainee, watched and listened to Paul closely.

- After a season of training, Paul released Timothy to do with others what he had seen and heard Paul do.

- Timothy found and selected certain "reliable people" to train for spiritual ministry.

- After a season of training, Timothy was expected to release these reliable people so they could "teach others" in the manner in which they themselves were taught.

In this single verse Paul identifies four generations of disciples: (1) himself — the initial trainer, (2) Timothy — Paul's apprentice and son in the Lord, (3) reliable people — Paul's grandchildren in the Lord, and (4) others — Paul's great grandchildren in the Lord.

This is the pattern. Jesus modeled it. Paul copied it. And the church today needs equipping-leaders who will duplicate it!

Here is a final word of caution. Don't confuse *having meetings* with *developing ministers*. The church calendar is often stuffed, year after year, with one well-intended meeting after another. Organizing classes on discipleship and leadership development will do little good unless the leaders themselves know how to *touch, teach and train* people.

Always remember this: equipping people for ministry isn't about going through a book and answering questions. It's about relationships, passion, focus, determination and transformation. Following a curriculum is a good idea, but only as long as the major emphasis is kept on measurable personal growth and effective service for the Kingdom of God.

Now, with this introduction to *being* a disciple and *making* disciples, investigate some discipleship books and workbooks to find the one(s) that best fit your needs. Here are a few suggestions:

Disciple Shift by Jim Putman and Bobby Harrington with Robert E. Coleman (Zondervan).

Transforming Discipleship by Greg Ogden (Inter-Varsity Press).

The Master Plan of Evangelism by Robert E. Coleman (Baker).

Celebration of Discipline by Richard J. Foster (Harper One).

The Spirit of the Disciplines by Dallas Willard (Harper One).

Ten Questions to Diagnose Your Spiritual Health by Donald S. Whitney (NavPress).

Books by Stephen Swihart: *Spiritual Development, Doable Discipleship - Volumes 1 and 2, Intentional Discipleship,* and other titles, all available at www.Amazon.com.

God be with you (Matthew 28:19-20)!